This book was created by community members of the Central Valley during the 2020 COVID-19 Pandemic. This book is a reminder to eat good food, share your story with others and love like no tomorrow...

acknowledgements

This book was inspired by

ALEXANDRA SHANNON-RUBIO

Contributors to design and publishing

JOANNA ESPARZA
SAVANNAH WILLIAMS
MARIA TORRES

Thank you to each inspired Chef and each have person whom shared their story in this book.

eat, share, love

table of contents

eat

[ˈēt]

to consume gradually

Xiomara's French Toast

Chef Xiomara Huerta

ingredients

- Bread (Any Kind)
- Milk
- 2 Eggs
- Vanilla Extract
- Cinnamon
- Butter or Oil

instructions

- In a medium bowl mix the milk, eggs, vanilla extract, and cinnamon.
- It must be mixed well until the liquid looks dark yellow with a little brown.
- Pick how many pieces of bread you want.
- On a cutting board, cut the bread into triangles or half.
- Get a slice of bread and dip it into the mixture.
- Soak the bread for 15-20 seconds.
- Repeat dipping for all the bread slices.
- Make sure both sides of the bread slice are covered in the mixture.
- In a pan, melt butter or oil.
- Wait until the pan gets hot to cook the bread.
- Only cook the bread 5-10 minutes to prevent burning.
- Make sure when you are going to flip the bread, the side must be golden.
- Until both sides are golden, that means it is done cooking.

When your fresh French Toast is completely cooked, make sure to top it off with your favorite toppings, such as syrup or powdered sugar.

a note from the chef

My name is Xiomara Giselle Huerta, and I am 11 years old. I am from Modesto, California, and one of my favorite hobbies is cooking. I also enjoy riding my bike and spending time with my pets. Did you know that French Toast was created in the year 1871? I enjoy preparing French toast because it is easy to make. A few ingredients from the fridge and a few ingredients from the cabinet should do the trick. You won't have to worry about taking too long for a delicious breakfast. Let's begin to make this flavorsome dish.

Tofu Scramble

❧

Chef Jessica Riojas

ingredients

- Canola Oil
- Tofu (Extra Firm)
- Onions
- Potato's
- Peppers
- Avocado
- Pepper

instructions

- First, make sure the tofu is dried with a paper towel
- Then, cut the tofu into little squares, cut peppers, and potatoes
- Next, sauté the potatoes in a pan with a little canola oil
- Add in the tofu into the same pan
- Add in all veggies
- Lastly, add pepper or salt
- You can eat this with tortillas for a wrap or enjoy just by itself!

a note from the chef

Hi! I am a female living in the Central Valley who is finishing up my last year in college. I am a mom to a beautiful 3 year old daughter, Eden. I love to hike, eat, and explore. I love God . I chose this recipe because it is an inexpensive vegan meal that my toddler and I love to enjoy together!

Crock Pot Stuffed Peppers Soup

Chef Monica Johnson

ingredients

- 1 pound of browned ground beef or ground turkey
- 1/2 onion chopped (I used red onion, but any will do)
- 1/2 red pepper -chopped
- 1/2 green bell pepper -chopped
- 1 can diced tomatoes
- 14 oz can of tomato sauce
- 14 oz can of water
- 1 tsp of oregano
- 1 tsp garlic salt
- 1 tablespoon Worcestershire sauce
- 1 tsp pepper
- 2 cups cooked white rice (You can use brown rice if you prefer)

instructions

You are not going to believe how easy this recipe is to make.
It tastes like it took tons of work like stuffed peppers but I promise it's simple to create!

- First place everything (except the rice) in the crockpot
- Then stir to combine thoroughly
- Next cover and cook on low for 6 to 8 hours (4 to 6 hours on high)
- While the soup is in the crock pot, cook rice on the side.
- After this cook time, stir the crockpot stuffed peppers soup before serving
- The bell peppers will be soft and delicious.
- Spoon the soup into a bowl and top with a spoonful of the cooked rice

Enjoy!

a note from the chef

Hello my name is Monica Johnson. I am a Modesto native, happily married with two 12 year old boys. I love working with youth and young adults building them up physically, mentally, emotionally, financially and spiritually. My favorite things to do is go hiking, traveling, watching movies, game nights and hanging out with family/friends. I am very family oriented and love building memories with my family. One of those ways is always over food. It wasn't until my late 20's that I found a passion to try new recipes and expand me and my families taste buds. Family members are the most authentic and most honest 'critic-ers' you can ever have. One of our favorite recipes I found on Facebook, yes Facebook. It's called, " Stuffed Bell Pepper Soup". As a wife/mom, the crockpot is going to be your best friend. Prep the meal, slowly cook it, allow the savory aroma to fill your house & make everyone's stomachs growl and then serve. I am not a big soup person, but this takes your taste buds to the next level.

Mexican
Rice

Chef Nancy Williams

ingredients

- 2 cups of long grain rice
- 1 can of tomato sauce Pato brand (spicier taste) or Del Monte brand (regular taste)
- 2 cups of water
- 2 cups of chicken broth
- 1 tablespoon of oil
- 3 cloves of garlic
- A quarter of a bunch of cilantro
- A quarter of a white onion
- 1 whole jalapeño
- 1 teaspoon of salt
- 1 tablespoon of cumin

instructions

- Cut the garlic into small pieces and smash them (smash in a molcajete if you have one)
- Cut a quarter off of the cilantro bunch
- Cut the cilantro into small pieces
- Cut off a quarter of a white onion
- Heat oil in the pan for 2 mins
- Add the onions and rice
- Stir until the rice turns brown
- Add tomato sauce, 2 cups of Water, 2 cups of chicken broth, smashed garlic, cilantro, 1 whole Jalapeño, 1 teaspoon of salt, 1 tablespoon of cumin
- Bring to a boil, then
- Put it on low heat and simmer for 10 minutes
- Turn off stove and let sit for 5 minutes

Serve!

a note from the chef

My name is Nancy Williams. I am a hard working and giving lady. I've lived in Modesto for 50+ years. Over the years, I have had the opportunity to feed thousands of homeless people through the Good Samaritan Food Bank that I lead under the umbrella of my church, Revival Center. I now enjoy my days spending time with my dog babies, Kingston Michael and Valentine Princeton and my adorable grandson, Zayden King Jeremiah. I have cooked this rice for my husband Jeremiah Williams, my three children (Savannah Maria, Joshua and Jeremiah Michael) and my family and friends for many years. Everyone loves my rice! It's a staple in the relationships at my table.

13

Campi's Spaghetti

Chef Cathy Risch

ingredients

- 2 tablespoons of olive oil
- 2 teaspoons of italian seasoning
- 2 bay leaves
- 1 teaspoon of oregano
- 5 teaspoons of salt
- 1 teaspoon of black pepper
- 1 tablespoon of sugar
- 1/2 pound of sliced Cremini mushrooms
- 1 large onion
- 6 garlic cloves
- 4 cans of tomato sauce
- 2 cans of tomato paste
- 2 cans of water
- 1 cup of burgundy wine
- 4 Italian sausage (mild)
- 1 1/2 lb of ground chuck (hamburger meat)
- 1 lb of spaghetti noodles

Note: if you do not eat meat, you can exclude it

instructions

- Prep dice (cut) the onions, mince (chop up and mash) the garlic cloves
- Cut each Italian sausage link into 6 pieces
- Add 2 tablespoons of olive oil into a pan
- Add the Italian sausage, ground beef and onions
- Cook until the onions are translucent (see through)
- Add garlic and mushrooms to the meat. Cook for 1 minute
- Add the italian seasoning,, oregano, 4 teaspoons of salt, and black pepper, cook for 1 minute
- Add the cans of tomato sauce and tomato paste
- Fill 2 empty tomato sauce cans with water and pour them in
- Add the burgundy wine
- Add sugar and bay leaves
- Cover the pan and let it simmer for 1 hour
- In a separate pan add the spaghetti noodles and a teaspoon of salt, boil for 20 minutes

Serve Pour Spaghetti sauce and meat on top of the noodles

Optional: add olives and cheese, mix it up and put it in the oven on 350 degrees for 10 minutes

a note from the chef

I was born and raised in Oakland, CA. I have lived in the Central Valley for 30 years of my life. I have suffered domestic violence, loss, rejection and health issues. Nonetheless, cooking was my peace of mind and my way to connect to others. Over the years, I have cooked for over 30,000 people. This recipe is dear to me because I have an Italian father. He would make spaghetti for us all the time; at least 3 times a week. We would also have our extended family join us. So at 13 years old, I learned how to cook this specialty spaghetti.

Now, I am blind so I hope this recipe can live on through you.

15

Parmesan Sage Crusted Pork Chops & Apple Slaw with Pearl Cous-Cous

Chef Cass Mellow

ingredients

- Pork chops
- House made Garlic Butter
- Fresh Sage
- Parmesan
- Egg
- Italian breadcrumbs
- Apple Slaw: Julienned Green Granny Smith Apples
- Mixed leafy greens
- Pickled Red Onion
- Edible flowers for color
- Orange vinaigrette
- Pearl Cous-Cous: Israeli Cous-Cous
- Shallots
- Water
- Salt
- White Pepper
- Agave Syrup
- Red Wine Vinegar

instructions

- Season 2 pork chops with salt and set out to rest in room temp for 30min
- Prepare batter for Chops: put breadcrumbs in one bowl with finely chopped sage and fresh parmesan or grated parmesan and mix together evenly. Set aside.
- Take two eggs and beat thoroughly. Set aside.
- Vinaigrette: one orange, juice and strain seeds out, one teaspoon of lemon juice, and half a cup of oil and 1/3 teaspoon of salt. Mix thoroughly.
- Take one Granny Smith Apple and slice into four pieces creating a square core in which is waste. Slice Apple long wise, turn on side and slice into sticks. Take small handful of mixed greens and two pinches of pickled onions and mix in a bowl with a pinch of salt and orange vinaigrette.
- Mix slaw and vinaigrette together when about to plate.
- Cous-Cous: toast two shallots chopped then add 1 cup of cous cous in large sauce pan and brown on medium heat with two tablespoons of olive oil. Once browned add 2 cups of water with 1 tablespoon of salt and let simmer like rice, covered, when 2/3 of water has been reduced add 2 tablespoons of red wine Vinegar and 2 tablespoons of agave syrup. Let finish simmering until it starts to crisp up a bit then turn off.
- Brown garlic butter in pan on low and coat pork chops in egg then breadcrumb mixture. Turn pan on medium high and let it get hotter for two minutes then add Chops. Turn after 4 minutes. Cook the remaining side for another 3-4 minutes and then turn off but still basking the chops in butter with a spoon for another two.
- Let rest, slice and lay on top of AppleSlaw, drizzle remaining glaze on top.

Plate cous-cous in a ring or however you feel is aethetically pleasing.
Enjoy!

a note from the chef

I'm an aspiring Chef growing in the industry as well as a Photography for many things. This recipe is one I learned while Working for a Michelin star chef. He had me recreate it in my own way so it was , in fact, my first signature dish ever attempted.

Cranberry

Salad

Dessert

〜

Chef Stella Ureno

ingredients

- 1 large carton of fresh heavy whipping cream
- 1 container of Cranberry/Orange relish (from Trader Joe's- sold during the holiday season)
- 1 20 oz can of crushed Pineapple (drain the juice)
- 1 bag of miniature marshmallows

instructions

- Combine all the ingredients in a large mixing bowl and delicately fold together until well mixed.
- Refrigerate overnight to allow marshmallows and all the ingredients to absorb the whip creme.

Serve the next day and enjoy!

a note from the chef

I'm a retired educator, community volunteer, wife and mom to our little dog Mimi. I love rescue dogs and consider myself an animal advocate and support many organizations that help protect nature and our environment. For many years I worked with students at K-12 schools, at colleges and universities throughout the Central Valley and Central Coast as a college recruiter, teacher, academic advisor, counselor, program manager, and administrator. I'm a life learner and lover of art, culture, history, and socializing with family & friends. I like to visit museums and historical sites. I also love to travel world wide. I have visited numerous countries including the UK, Austria, Croatia, Egypt, Italy, Peru, Russia, Spain, Sweden, and Turkey.
I chose this recipe because it was a recipe that my eldest sister Shirley used to make for our family gatherings during the holidays. I have fond memories of our family get togethers at my Mom and Dads house in Sanger, CA. We would always get together for the holidays like on Thanksgiving, Christmas, & Easter and share a wonderful holiday meal with many wonderful desserts that she would make & bring over. She passed away a few years ago, so I like to continue making this recipe because it reminds me of her and our family get togethers. I believe that keeping family traditions alive are important and it's a positive way of honoring and remembering our loved ones that have passed away.

Chocolate Chip Scones

Chef Alexandra Rubio

ingredients

- 1 bag of Chocolate Chips (I prefer to use semi-sweet but you can use any you would like)
- 1 tsp Apple Cider Vinegar
- 1/3 cup of Milk
- 1 cup of Butter
- 1/4 cup plus 2 tsp of sugar
- 3 eggs
- 3 cups of flour
- 1 tsp baking powder

instructions

- Pre-Heat oven to 350 degrees F
- Put vinegar in a measuring cup and add enough milk to make 1/3 cup
- Next, put the butter and sugar in a large mixing bowl and beat with an electric mixer. (If you don't have an electric mixer, mixing by hand will work as well)
- Your mixture should be pale and fluffy
- Add all 3 eggs to your mixture and keep mixing until mixture is fully combined
- Add milk
- Add flour and baking powder slowly, and keep mixing until fully combined
- Lastly, add chocolate chips and mix
- Roll dough into medium sized balls and place on a cookie sheet
- Refrigerate for 15 minutes
- Bake for 15 minutes, then decrease the oven temperature to 325 degrees F and bake for 10-15 minutes.

Let cool, and enjoy!

a note from the chef

Growing up, one of my favorite memories was cooking with my grandparents. It was our time to really bond together. My grandparents both love to cook/bake and they are both AMAZING at it. After learning from the two best cooks I know. I started to experiment with my own recipes. A huge crowd pleaser was these famous chocolate chip scones. These are the easiest and most perfect recipe to bake when you need a quick idea. This recipe is sure-fire way to impress anyone with your baking skills!

21

share

['sher]

to partake of, use, experience,
occupy, or enjoy with others

> To the world you may be one person; but to one person, you may be the world.
>
> –Dr. Seuss

Bonnie Joy Arbuckle

age 46

How did She Became improve your lifestyle?

B: She Became has helped me focus on the positive, value myself much more, and teach my daughter to value herself more.

How has She Became helped you increase your level of self-love?

B: Being involved with She Became has awakened my value in this world, and that what I do can affect and inspire others.

In moments of self-doubt or adversity, how do you build yourself back-up?

B: When this happens, I take a time out and regroup. We all have those moments of weakness, and it's okay; you just can't unpack and live there in those feelings. I deal with those feelings and try to regain focus on my mission and all that I have to gain by keeping my eye on the prize.

What is your advice to girls and women?

B: Don't allow others to define your value or self-worth. You are an amazing individual with your own gifts to share with the world, and you will shine in your own special way.

Which of your traits are you most proud of?

Humorous, Organized & Outgoing

24

What characteristics do you admire most in other women?

Y: Kind, caring, and loving.

Share your biggest overall lesson you have learned in life.

Y: Trust in others and trust in myself.

How did She Became improve your lifestyle?

Y: By helping me get out of my comfort zone and talk to other people.

Name a woman, whom you admire or look up to. In one sentence, share her character traits.

Y: My mother, Adriana. She is a wonderful person, an amazing mom, cares about other people, an excellent business woman, and the nicest person. I'm glad that she is my mom.

What is your advice to girls and women?

Y: Follow your dreams and never give up on anything, because **YOU CAN DO IT!**

Yzelia Rosa Garcia

age 15

"
If you can't fly, then run.
If you can't run, then walk.
If you can't walk, then crawl,
but by all means,
keep moving

–Martin Luther King Jr.
"

What is your advice to girls and women?

D: Be good to yourself; the world needs you.

Debra Dia Herrera

age 56

> " Check yourself, before you wreck yourself

–Unknown

How has She Became inspired you?

D: It inspired me to be the difference that I want to see.

Which of your traits are you most proud of?

D: My ability to laugh at my mistakes and still have a desire to take risks.

Share your biggest overall lesson you have learned in life.

D: You can't change your past, no matter how many times you replay the monologue.

In moments of self-doubt or adversity, how do you build yourself back up?

A: I have learned to be a little nicer to myself. I have to remind myself that I am and will continue to learn, and I have learned to be okay with that. It's okay to make mistakes as long as I am learning from them. Never take a lesson for granted, no matter how embarrassing, sad, or difficult it may be. It can always make you better.

What is your advice to girls and women?

A: Seek and help others. We will all need help at one point or another, and that's okay. Lean on others when needed, but be sure to return the favor. Nothing is ever final. Life is a rollercoaster, and it includes sadness, fear, happiness, love and so much more. So buckle up, be safe, but most of all, enjoy the ride!

"

Love all, trust a few, do wrong to none.

-William Shakespeare

Adriana Garcia

age 39

Name a woman, whom you admire or look up to. In one sentence, share her character traits.

A: I admire all women in general. Our ability to love, re-invent, and create life is remarkable. My mother has been one of the most influential women in my life. She is the strongest, most courageous and loving woman I know. She has always held me be accountable and corrected me when I'm wrong.

> " I'd rather be hated for being myself, than to be someone else.
>
> -Unknown

Xiomara Giselle Huerta

age 11

What is your advice to girls and women?

X: Be yourself; don't be afraid to say what you mean.

Name a woman, whom you admire or look up to. In one sentence, share her character traits.

X: I admire Hwsa because she is bold, fearless, fierce and free-spirited.

How has She Became helped you move forward in your life?

X: By helping me have confidence when speaking in front of people.

Share your biggest lesson you have learned in life.

X: Love yourself. You never walk alone. Hard work is the key.

How has She Became inspired you?

X: To not be intimidated by age and make sure that my voice is being heard.

28

What is your advice to girls and women?

D: To follow your dreams; we only have one life to live. Make sure you do something you love that fills you with passion and joy.

How did She Became improve your lifestyle?

D: She Became reminded me that there is always someone who needs to hear your story. I didn't have a mentor growing up. She Became has allowed me to share my gifts and talents with it's members.

Name a woman, whom you admire or look up to. In one sentence, share her character traits.

D: I always look up to Frida Kahlo for inspiration. Her tenacity to find a way to make art through her pain is admirable

In moments of self-doubt or adversity, how do you build yourself back up?

D: When I have a moment that is full of challenges, I remember that there may be someone attached to me, waiting for me, to do the thing I am trying to do. Let me explain. If I have a goal that I have been working on, and I am unexpectedly presented with obstacles, what helps me to overcome that, is to think about all the people who may benefit from me achieving my goal. All the youth that I can inspire in telling the story of the challenge I was faced with and overcame or of the person who needs to be inspired by hearing my story of meeting this goal, and maybe they could say, " because she did it so can I."

Domenica Escatel

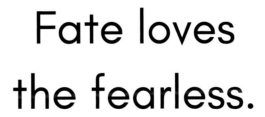

Fate loves the fearless.

–James Russell Lowell

What is your advice to girls and women?

N: Be kind and patient with yourself! Be careful what you listen to, watch, and read. What goes inside your ears will make its way to your heart and then to your mind.

Natasha Matsipura

"

Commit your actions to the Lord, and your plans will succeed.

- Proverbs 16:3

How have you turned your mistakes into opportunities?
N: My mistakes have taught me to stop and think before I do anything and be patient with myself. Allow myself to think about the next move or just stand back and see what something will turn into. God has always made all things work out for my good and His glory.

How can we empower others more?

N: Just be more understanding. Less judgemental. Allowing room for mistakes and not setting self-limits.

What does success mean to you?

N: Success, to me, means being round by myself. Taking things one day at a time and celebrating my accomplishments, but reflecting on my fails and trying to learn and grow from them. It can be the smallest thing to how I see myself in 5 years from now.

How has She Became inspired you?

A: To be more involved with family and friends, and enjoy the time you have together.

How did She Became improve your lifestyle?

A: It helps me move forward in my life knowing I am helping others, and I love to help.

What is your advice to girls and women?

A: Stay strong you got this.

In moments of self-doubt or adversity, how do you build yourself back up?

A: I tell myself, "no one has a say in me because I am the only one who knows how I feel."

Alyssa Gomez

Never give up

How did She Became improve your lifestyle?

A: By having me be more proactive with my community, and it has shown me to be more confident and outgoing.

How has She Became helped you increase your level of self-love?

A: Joanna (the Founder of She Became) is so supportive and nice. She has shown me a lot about self-love and not caring so much about what others think.

Adriana Barriga

"

I tell myself, "no one has a say in me because I am the only one who knows how I feel."

Mother Theresa

With all that you have experienced and learned through She Became, how will the principles and lessons be applied to your personal or professional life?

A: I handle both areas better because of the help of She Became.

How did She Became improve your lifestyle

A: By awakening my passion for helping others and paying close attention to our young community. She Became has also **impacted my relationship with my three daughters** who joined the She Became experience with me. Now, all four of us love helping and participating in their meetings, volunteering, and my daughters and I see our community from a different view.

32

What is your advice to girls and women?

D: I would say; please don't worry if you're good enough for this person and that person. Just be the person YOU want to be because, in the end, it comes to self-love, and you can't have that if you're trying to please other people. So love yourself!!!

Share your biggest overall lesson you have learned in life

D: The biggest lesson I learned in life so far is that you NEVER know what someone else is going through. So, be kind and treat them how you would want to be treated.

In moments of self-doubt or adversity, how do you build yourself back up?

D: I have moments of self-doubt and adversity often, but I never stay in those moments for long because I build myself back up by remembering my self-worth, and I can do anything I put my mind to. I just can't give up.

How did She Became improve your lifestyle?

D: By having me be more proactive with my community, and it has shown me to be more confident and outgoing.

Davey Gomez

"Treat people how you want to be treated."

What do you believe our world needs more of...

J: The understanding of self. Listening... truly listening to our fellow people, to embrace each others' differences and celebrate what makes us different. I believe the world needs to learn how to collaborate, communicate, persevere, find your passion/purpose, etc.

Please send a loving, positive, and encouraging message to girls and women

J: Keep your head up! You are strong, beautiful, amazing, and one of a kind

In what ways do you serve your community

J: I am a mentor for the community program - Project Uplift. Project Uplift is a program designed to help young men and women in the understanding of life skills, self-worth, respect of others and community, leadership skills, etc. I am also the First Vice President of the Stanislaus 1048 NAACP. Furthermore, I am the host and creator of the podcast series "I ON MODESTO". This podcast focuses on the positive aspects of community members, leaders, and organizations. The podcast also points out the struggles, challenges, and problems within the Modesto Community. Lastly, I am a motivational speaker in my speaking initiative/business - The House Of Redemption (THOR).

What is your message to our community?

" Don't waste time because, in essence, time is wasting you!! "

We would like to thank you for investing into She Became either with your time, finances, or by helping us move our mission forward. What made you believe in our vision and mission

J: Joanna Esparza and her team's tireless drive inspires me to push on with my dreams. Joanna started with an idea, and through the efforts of her and her team, incredible strides have been made in the empowerment of women in the Modesto community. Joanna is a beacon of tenacity and true grit.

John Isaiah Griffin

34

In what ways do you serve your community?

D: I manage a program for youth ages 17 to 24 in our community. I work directly with these young people through case management, mentoring, career development, and assisting youth with life management.

What made you serve your community in this way?

D: Young adults and teens are my passion. I believe God calls to ministry in many different forms. I believe God has placed me in this position to reach as many young adults as possible. My hope is for these young people to not only get a good job, but will eventually find Christ.

What is your message to our community?

D: We have a great community, but we also have a lot of struggling people in our community. Hope is free, and many people have that hope that needs to be shared with those around them, not caring about who, what, or why they are where they are.

We would like to thank you for investing into She Became either with your time, finances, or by helping us move our mission forward. What made you believe in our vision and mission?

D: First, you have to believe in the people who have the vision -- that was easy. I knew the vision and mission would fall into place.

Please send a loving, positive, and encouraging message to girls and women

D: More women and girls need to remember how valuable they are and not allow society, men, social media, or even their peers to determine their worth and purpose.

Dustin Pack

Hope is free, and many people have that

In what ways do you serve your community?

B: For 16 years working at Modesto Junior College, I helped students from all walks of life learn to believe in themselves and what they could do in this world by graduating college. Today, I serve our community through my portion with Love Stanislaus by helping people in need connect to resources that can assist them.

Share a positive and encouraging message to our community

B: You have two choices in life. You can exist, or you can live.

Please send a loving, positive, and encouraging message to girls and women

B: Value yourself and your contributions, and never allow anyone to let you feel less or tell you that you can't do something.

What is your message to our community?

Anything is possible if you believe

We would like to thank you for investing into She Became either with your time, finances, or by helping us move our mission forward. What made you believe in our vision and mission

B: She Became represents everything we need in our community. They saw a need and took the initiative to want to make a difference. That's easy to get behind and believe in.

Bryan Justin Marks

What do you believe our world needs more of...

B: Faith in God, Faith in each other, and Faith in ourselves.

Name a woman, whom you admire or look up to. In one sentence, share her character traits.

M: Joanna Esparza, the Founder of She Became, is the woman I most admire. The character traits I admire most about her is that she inspires others to embrace their true beauty, is determined to spread She Became to others, and her ability to be vulnerable and share her story with others makes her a woman that I look up to.

How did She Became improve your lifestyle?

M: By reminding me to stay true to myself. I learned how to love myself and spread that love to others. I remind myself that I am beautiful, I am enough, I am brave, I am loved, and I hold the power to my own future.

What is your advice to girls and women?

M: My advice to other girls and women is to always be true to yourself and know your worth. Don't settle for less because you think it's not possible; settle for more because you are always worth more than you think. In relationships with people, goals, and with yourself, know that you deserve more.

Share your biggest overall lesson you have learned in life.

M: The biggest overall lesson that I have learned in life is that mistakes are lessons. We don't wake up being perfect at everything. We learn and grow from the things that happen to us, rather than taking them as bad experiences. For example, instead of saying, "I made a mistake," I can say, "I learned how to _____." This is important because mistakes are inevitable and will happen. A change of mindset has been a great life learned skill.

Maribel Ibarra

"Vulnerability is not about winning or losing. It's having the courage to show up even when you can't control the outcome."

In moments of self-doubt or adversity, how do you build yourself back up?

M: I first take deep breathes in moments of doubt. It helps that I remind myself that I am only human, so this is natural; however, taking a moment to step back and breathe allows me to reevaluate a situation. I also reach out to a close friend, Florentina Medina, or my closest family member Monica Pedroza to talk. Sharing my feelings with them also helps me center.

Name a woman, whom you admire or look up to. In one sentence, share her character traits.

B: My mother, as an undocumented woman, has worked hard every day and night to give her kids a good life.

How has She Became inspired you?

B: She Became has helped me understand that even on my worst days, I can be successful.

Brisa Antunez Mendoza

66

Forget the failures, keep the lessons.

99

How has She Became helped you move forward in your life?

B: With She Became, I have become motivated to focus on my future and be more organized.

Which of your traits are you most proud of?

B: If life brings me down, I get up and face my problems, and I never give up.

What is your advice to girls and women?

B: You are powerful; don't ever let anyone bring you down

Please send She Became a positive and encouraging message for the years to come.

A: **STAY**

STRONG. YOU

ARE WORLD

CHANGERS!

Send a loving, positive, and encouraging message to girls and women.

A: Love yourself.
You are unique all in your own way.

We would like to thank you for investing into She Became either with your time, finances, or by helping us move our mission forward. What made you believe in our vision and mission? *

A: The helpfulness and confidence they give young woman to let them know they are loved and appreciated.

What is your message to our community?

My message to the people of Stanislaus is to continue to support local non profits. Because they are the only ones looking for our neighbors our children locally and that is what matters that we take care of ourselves.

Armando Raya

Continue to love and serve.

I contribute to SHE BECAME because...
A: What made me serve with She Became was because I have a young daughter that is turning a teenager very soon. I know at her age the world could be cruel. I would love her at her age to know that there are people that care for her physically and emotionally.

Which of your traits are you most proud of?

A: I am most proud of my hard work and patience. Although patience has been a learning curve for me, it has been a trait that I am really proud to have attained.

In moments of self-doubt or adversity, how do you build yourself back up?

A: I have learned to ground myself using techniques and coping skills, and I turn to people close to me and whom I trust

In moments of self-doubt or adversity, how do you build yourself back up?

A: That not everything is handed to us, we have to work hard, stay strong, and be resilient.

Angela Ramirez

"
Don't be afraid. Be focused. Be determined. Be hopeful. Be empowered.
"

How has She Became helped you increase your level of self-love?

A: She Became is always promoting self-love and self-care, which is something that I used to be bad at doing, and I used to think it was selfish. Now, I focus on taking care of myself and loving myself in the process.

With all that you have experienced and learned through She Became, how will the principles and lessons be applied to your personal or professional life?

A: I will continue to connect with other women around me and, eventually, I want to be someone that can share my experiences and wisdom with others.

40

What is your advice to girls and women?

A: **When you think you don't matter, remember, you MATTER because you belong with She Became and we are family.**

Has She Became helped you in increasing your self-love or self-esteem? If yes, please explain how

A: Indeed, I chose to love myself instead of seeing the unloved parts of me. I cherish the beautiful peace I have after acceptance of one's own body.

How have you turned your mistakes into opportunities?

A: I used to dwell on them, but now I see them as a lesson, and **they give me motivation to keep pushing forward.**

What does success mean to you?

Determination: if you put your mind to do it, you will learn to master it.

Blanca Yadira Munguia Corona

If nothing is going right, turn left. If nothing is good on the left side, keep moving straight; the roads are windy for a reason. Don't let crazy roads determine your stirring.

How did She Became improve your lifestyle?

She Became improved my lifestyle in many ways by showing me what it is like to be supported by many inspiring, and motivated women not only in my local area, but all around me. I gained the confidence of wanting my voice to be heard, and now I want to help other women find their voice!

Kayla Salazar Contreras Martinez

"Pray For Guidance," "Trust The Process," "Value The Outcome," and "Keep on Smiling." -Vianett

What is your advice to girls and women?

Know their **worth** because nobody knows what they deserve more than themselves. Each girl and woman is capable of anything and will go as far as they take themselves.
Work hard for their **DREAMS** and **harder for their GOALS**, but they also should not forget that the recipe to a healthy mindset is **self-care**.

What were your initial thoughts about She Became?

A: Initially, I thought She Became was going to be about women empowerment, and I was not wrong. I never realized how empowering it feels to be supported by a community of strong independent, hard working women until I was introduced to She Became.

Has She Became helped you in increasing your self-love or self-esteem? If yes, please explain how.

A. She became helped me see how loved I am. With realizing how important mental health is, I began taking care of my state of mind by surrounding myself with positive thinking, hard working, humble and caring women that I look up to.

Share your biggest overall lesson you have learned in life.

The biggest overall lesson I've recently learned was that it is okay to put myself first. I've gotten hurt plenty of times for putting other people's feelings before mine. I allowed people to change the way I think and feel about myself. Now that I found my voice, I can finally hear myself out and speak up so I can be heard.

love

[ˈləv]
strong affection for another
arising out of kinship or
personal ties

A LOVE LETTER TO OUR COMMUNITY
& OUR WHY BEHIND THE SCENES

Eat Share Love was held for the very first time out of a need to serve our underserved youth during the holidays. Often we don't think much about the teens who will not experience a loving and comforting holiday dinner. With limited resources we began to plan a day in which we would prepare and serve a home cooked meal while sharing some quality time with local teens.

Our very first year we to served 17 teens both girls and boys. It was the best feeling to be able to show our youth that there are adults that care about them and they are never forgotten.

Each year after that we began to dream bigger and began to invite the community to participate. We invited parents and professionals to join in Eating with, Sharing, and Loving on our youth. As you may know everyone receives and gives love in different ways. During this program you would experience all five love languages. In other words, we would spend quality time together, serve, hug, celebrate, recognize our volunteers, and make long lasting memories.

In 2020 we decided to innovate how we can send this message to your home. You will find amazing recipes that were shared by local community members and that were chosen with love. Each Chef shares a bit about why it's special to them. Our hope is that you enjoy each recipe.

We also invited girls and women to share their personal story with She Became and what inspires them.

Love is expressed in many ways and we had some incredible people be a part of our journey and that includes some great men that have either donated their time, finances, or resources to be a part of our success.

We truly hope that you enjoy this gesture of Eat Share Love

she became

46

A LOVE LETTER FROM OUR FOUNDER

Dear Beloved Community Member,

As we prepare to publish and share this incredible book that has been written by, prepared by, and accomplished by community members, I hope that you find inspiration to continue to grow into who you are destined to be. As our mission continues to evolve, adapt, and expand around this community and onto others, we invite you to become a part of this community and mission at She Became.

You have been nothing more than a supportive and blessing to many around you. Whether that has been through our organization or simply in the lives of those around you. Girl, Boy, Woman, or Man, you have been made and planted into this time for only a reason that you can discover and fulfil. It is up to you to discover that reason and then begin to live it out. In a time when we are challenged to dream yet scared to believe in our dream, let me tell you to believe in that dream and chase it! Chase it like no one is around you and protect it with it all that you have!

When we can not only believe in the dream but then chase after it and protect it, it is when all of the magic begins. Little by little, you will see changes, challenges, tests, and all of the opportunities that come your way. However this is what makes that dream come true and what makes it so worth it.

Beauty lies in the story that you get to tell of how you got to where you are today. Beauty lies in the smiles and the tears. Beauty lies in the laughs and in the sorrows. Beauty lies within you.

Allow this book to be the beginning of your journey of seeking, discovering, and becoming all that you can be and more. We never stop being and we never stop giving until we have fulfilled our purpose.

With Love,

Joanna Esparza
Founder of she became

47

Special shout-out to Mentors

Rose
Don
Pat
Ben
Liz
Juan
Tyra
Rudy
Rosa
Kathy
Linda
Sarah
Debra
Ashley
Dustin
Glenda
Teresa
Tanya
Ilse
Edward
Yvonne
Meriel
Linda
Robin
Marilyn
Suzanne
Dawn
Cherie
Sandy
Sophie
Laurie
Pastor Chuck
Monique
Michelle
Bryan
Jesus
Brady
Analisa
Rebecca
Cynthia
Nancy Williams
Jeremiah Williams
Cathy Risch
Marie Harrison
Terri Panelle
Morjan Mohammed
Mrs. Johnson
Sadi Munguia
Queen Rivera
Hector Garcia
Mrs. Johnson

Words that come to mind when thinking about She Became...

Authenticity
Community
Empowering
Empowerment
Hope
Inspirational
Sisterhood
Revolution
Authenticity
Growth
Beauty
Helpful
Effective
Powerful
Inclusive
Community

48

Reflections

This a reminder that our world needs more of you and what you can contribute. Reflect on your life and respond accordingly.

	I contribute in this area everyday by	I can improve in this area by
Love		
Empathy		
Morality		
Connection		
Acceptance		
Connection		
Forgiveness		
Goal Digger		
Kindness		
Generosity		
Understanding		
Compassion		
Unity		
She Became		

A Love Letter to myself...

A Love Letter to my future self...

A Love Letter to my community...

A space to write down all the things
you are grateful for...

A space to write down your dreams...

A space to write down your dreams...

A space to write down your thoughts...

A space to write down your thoughts...

A space to write down your future goals...

A space to write down your future goals...

A space to be free and let go...

A space to be free and let go...

A space take action...

A space take action...

A space to give myself permission to...

A space to give myself permission to...

A space to forgive

.

A space to move on...

the following pages are intended for you to write your story

you are powerful

You are in a chapter of your everlasting story.
The chapters are still being written...

keep going. keep believing. keep being you

CA ♥   ♥ GA

Invest into the lives of
girls and women through she became

WWW.SHEBECAME.COM I @SHEBECAME209

ISBN: 9798494707307

MAKE A ONE TIME OR MONTHLY MONETARY GIFT

VISIT OUR WEBSITE OR CONTACT SHE BECAME TO LEARN MORE

SHE BECAME IS A 501(C)(3) NONPROFIT ORGANIZATION

Made in the USA
Monee, IL
22 October 2021

5addc278-5483-4d04-8fc3-bff442ed76c7R01